THE DEER
ON THE FREEWAY

Ray Smith

Dakota Press
1973

University of South Dakota, Vermillion, South Dakota 57069

ACKNOWLEDGMENTS

A number of these poems appeared first in *South Dakota Review,*
Southern Humanities Review, Poetry, Poetry Claremont, Quetzal,
Steelhead, and *Tempora.*

CONTENTS

UNPOEM FOR M

How is it at your ocean?
Here I have carried your letters next to me
and pillowed my head each night in San Francisco
above your simple note "Good night."

There is only you. The city vibrates
through sun wind freshness. Clouds from the ocean
hang on its higher hills. On Haight Street
the Summer of Love, the flower people
walk in their separate festivals of costume
with bells and flowers. Tiny bookstores
are crammed with poems.

Here on the last hills before the ocean
there is only you.

THE DEER
ON THE FREEWAY

THE DEER ON THE FREEWAY

Not thyme, not ponderosa
that harsh scent.
Not waters rifting
that onrunning sound.
Not skein of grass and pine cones
that cold footing.

The weave of something antlered
in slicing light
across embankments as the engines power
a freeway curve. Headlamps momently prowl
its tossing hesitance,
swerve on the embankment, curve
along the concrete slope.
Wild pulse trapped, hooves drum concrete
forth, back, before the plunge
into swiveling beams—

JOLT   that smashed the deer
back through harsh scent
onrunning sound
footlessness.

MOUNTAIN CLOUDS

Clouds' tufty big brooms freely sweeping
prow on, hearts' high rises veering
along steep windflow of the San Gabriel crests:
uproiling vapor, Rockies of white air,
nimbus of sundrawn water, tumult's ringlets,
cumulus barrows, covey of phoenixes,
salvos of the wind's cannonade,
cattle of sunset, daybreak's cormorants.
They lift and lure as if to seize rock talons,
mouth abrupt wind above toylike perspectives.
Where it is early they fly and flow
and day's accounts blow out to sea
rags for cavorting gulls.

MOUNTAIN WATER
(for my daughters)

Each to each
the being-eye refracted
on the universal wing and crawl
of our immortal hike.
Exaltation of air.
Northward clear San Gabriels,
eastward ranges misted
under flocked clouds.
A cup of mountain water
proof that heights are there.

ABSENCE

Mountains tighten their shadows
where we were.
Ocean air retracts the prone light.

Acrid brush odor climbs this headland
where purple vine flowers
bob toward the cold vastness.

Westward the sun's wand
sweeps tumults of sea.
The heart catches for heat withdrawn.

COAST RAIN

At corners headlights waver,
fix beams, ride
on watermuted tires
tunneling dark aside.

Importunate needs
gust upon eye and ear.
All night a rushing wind
quickens the air.

Drowsing I hear once more
your rain-hastened feet
near day as watery lamps
gleam in the street.

L. A. BLUES

I walk at loose ends
Sunset or Santa Monica
asking alms of darkness
past standby citizens
and quickfry eateries.
Cruising lights beat
like jukeboxes on the eye.
Most of my life is over.
I have come near the time
of obedient ears
only to hear alone.

LEAVING THE COAST

Goodbye seafaring Grandfather spilled
like grain into the tense
under pull of the bay's immense water
as you had willed. Ocean light tips,
the blue stretch slackens where bobbing gulls
strutted water and pipers blinked
thin incessant legs behind outrunning combs.
The tide knocks. Shrouded by tenuous tall air
I watch too late by this wind-treadled cradle
to see it sift your funeral ashes down.

MAY MORNING

Air introjected with plum
odor incommensurate and surprising
pierces the nude senses,
hybrid of sight and smell
May's chameleon light
brimming tenderness for essaying things,
sourceless yet ripe as though
a golden planet struck and twinned our own.

THE FALLS IN MAY

Water cloddering
over falls escarpment
to the valley plunge
a weightfoot look away.
Clouds coast the sky floor.

Leathern lap of bats
around the flowering crab.
Sound without voice
and light unseen
dilate an unbound air.

OLD APPLE TREES

The unpruned beldames of the grass
each brimming like a gourd with shade
shook baffling twig interstices
against the summer light and made
the most of small dark, holding all they won.
Yet early each had eagerly drunk the sun.

BURNED BY A STAR

Burned by a star
curled waves run
out of cold depths
retrieved by siring sun.

A planet spitted
below slant fire
turns beyond retrieval
about its brood star.

THE NEW DAYS

Old age is the Rabbi.
See him groping
A father figure down the past's long ghetto,
Shameful beard and obsolescent clothing.

Diminishing in squalor of rejection
Move the ancients we deny.
Old men's infirmities are just.
Oil the machines and let the candles die.

WRITING POEMS

Writing poems that do not want to die
but seek a home among American silences

wait in the west by mesa walls in geometric shade
or rush to a vacant Iowa town at night
where streets run into cornfields' dry small clashings

walk a Pacific beach where heaving seas flex
over a heavy curtsey of fronds.

THE HOVER

This the hover, height reached,
end of wingsweep and soar,
stasis of time and wheel-turn.
Updraft or downdraft only
affect sheer curve before fall.
Only in age
the height's wonder returns.
Here in the air's drift
at wingsweep's end
only silent pause
after the uprush,
only perceptible
the failing glide
slow from the pivot,
earth in view, slowly
earth-return coming.

BAS-RELIEF AT HILDESHEIM

Thunder resounded in the garden.
Adam, one hand over his nakedness
pointed at Eve who cowering pointed
toward a coiled suppleness.
The lines bearing their burden
exit upon sorrow time-attainted.

Finding at the life-core seed
of a procreant divisive need
each had stricken the other's innocence.
To act beyond the self was to assume
mysteries of perpetual consequence
which time could bring to fruit but never redeem.

CAMPING IN THE BLACK HILLS
(for Rudy Johnson)

Two deer bound along the fence
thirty yards from camp
seeking a way to water.
We watch them pass and return
on slender legs like springs
to vanish in thick brush.
Earth exhalation rises into coolness
as the rigid burning disc descends
afloat in space behind straight pillars of pine.
Musk of rock moss, ferns, our balsam smoke
twines in the breeze freshets.

VISITING
ABERDEEN, SOUTH DAKOTA
(for my father)

A redbrick owly old museum:
cases of beadeyed posturing furs;
isinglass-windowed coal stove
dark within as an abandoned mineshaft;
a longribboned blue bonnet
hung from a laddered chair;
a scrolled hand mirror laid face down.

Aberdeen and the Jim River.
Wildfowl thick as berries then.
Nostril-grazing odor of alfalfa
canters on the breeze across shorn fields
in sunstung silence past the windbreak trees
that line tall silo slabs.
Sioux tipis near enough
for boys to bike to for quilled moccasins.

MY GRANDMOTHER

I never know you now
except when like an Easter you branch
along the dayspring of my veins
a total telling impulse
up out of memory's cartoons.

THE YELLOW LAMP

Grandma, your warm lamp's yellow light
shines to this distant evening.
You might be rocking
head bent above your needle
speaking of Sweden,
while darkness presses softly at the window
like a curling cat
eyes on the calm lamp glow.
Your fingers pause
as you look up and then resume.
Heavy in age you rock,
and I who lose the words
revive their murmur as hens chuk to quiet
and the home farm sleeps.

FOR TOM, FORMERLY
LIEUTENANT, AUS

Tom, remember
when we rode under the sea guns at Lorient
and they took Roser out
from that ambush cut to the spinal cord?

No more shot of Irish with him
tipped under the helmet shedding rain
after night map-briefing,
horizon flares like an *aurora borealis*
patching the low clouds with blinking light.

Do you still live?
Has it been any worse since then?

THREE LOVE SONGS FOR M

Come. Sinking Day

Come. Sinking day cries purple
clinging to earth's edge and over.
Awe spirals interstellar far,
an implausible way. May your body cover
often at such sinking and rise
my time-rung head
pressed mortally on your slim bones
home soft, comforted.

What Weather Makes

What weather makes, as you're not making me,
I peer over salmon streets and see
confirmed, for there hunched foothills lift
many haired up to blue draft.
So, but rumple sheeted night
clings to your rain hastened feet
as I clothe bare heart and go.
My weather is you.

This Is a Mortal Woman

This is a mortal woman beyond
graves. Her eyes are brown.
Time shall not lower her.
Light footsteps stun
all time's assay. Upon
a sunlit beach she moves her slender hands.
Her finger marks the day.
Intense noon stands.

TWO CONCORD POEMS

Emerson at Concord

In large and lucid Concord light
amply suspiring trees
enclose from wildness a garden west,
reason's preserve. Thoreau's rebellion
distant two miles may be paced out and back.
And here's our bridge with Freedom's presence
stately yet homespun, hominized.
Our scriptures quilled by elms
when evening comes while haying fields exhale
their sweetness brewed outside mortality
attest creation's first perpetual day.

At Walden

Item: square-headed nails and shanty boards.
Pond seen blue down slope in the sun sparkle
between pine boughs. Upon a level patch
the small cabin defined with corner posts.
Yeast in pocket and a borrowed book
to season lunch. Nearby a plot for beans.
Two miles from Concord by railway track
resting he looks across the axe at Walden,
blunt handyman for whom the classics buzz
insistent and domestic as the flies
about his hearthfire, Nature's counterpoint.
One man, who makes one suit of clothes his own
lest they wear him. The crudely hewn log upright
sole ornament of his fresh Doric day.

ROBINSON IN
TILBURY TOWN

Here I was born to verse
time's inward howl
down the slant town which wears
taciturnity as a cowl.
Stern lineage, scanted youth,
indentured hills, all teach
a flinty truth
faithful to frugal speech.

NOTE FOR HENRY JAMES

Velleities, careful discriminations.
Close upon earliest gas lamps carriage wheels
across smoothed cobbles. Furled umbrella cane.
Stair-tread surreptitiously worn.
The bell. Inquiring silence,
pulse quick beyond the draperies' decorum.
Why should she plunge to death
one hushed evening from her hushed balcony
into time's patina on the storied city?

A WINSLOW HOMER

Two fishermen loom from a stocky boat.
One leans in wet-slick helmet and oilskins
to draw through dense waves' weight
their herring-flurried floundering net.
Behind him veiled by dusk the other gleans
the sea where light's last viscous layer shines.

HOWELLS

"The smiling aspects of life"
were most American
before the Hudson River landscapes cracked
strike-rent and you saw
heartstruck the clawing cellarage.
But a polite Apollonian veil
still served. You helped draw it over
depths not tolerable, becoming
the socialist of Sunday lawns
with space for everyone, making prose cry
"The novel is downtown and I can't get there."

STEPHEN CRANE

You got to the marrow
all right and stayed there
sucking a ribbon of nourishment
becoming more and more yourself a bone.

NEW ENGLAND GENTRY

Rain gives the elms a ducking
comes to pour and peer
about your markers here
and windbent twigs are clicking.

The markers vertical once
have slipped through rain-eased gravel
askew in time's long sidle
like the tilt cap of a dunce.

They rate with rains' abatement
by slow steady subsidence
your declining presence
but prudential investment.

GARLIC AND SAPPHIRES: A TRIO

Literary V.I.P. at the Cocktail Hour

Poet: a European witness.
Think, we have reached no conclusions
When he bows into the readied room
(Aura of St. Praxed's Bishop's tomb).
Us he savors. Upright among the punch cups.

Carefully voiced regrets
Egresses and egrets.
I that was at his side was impelled therefrom
To think continually of these, of Those
Near the sun, near the snow. At the twilight hour
(Bringer of draymen to the pungent bar)
We have lost our passion who most need to keep it
Having learned how to care and not to care.

The Death of the Steeplejack

Part of the roof came tumbling from the eaves
Upon them on their doorstep in the dusk,
She saw in time and caught it. "Carl," she said
Hefting the fragment, "Carl, I am afraid
Jack's climbed his final steeple. He fell today—"
"Well?" he asked tartly, "What is it to us?
He's not my brother or yours. Nor uncle, neither."
A piece of drain-pipe missed them in the darkness
Tearing the whole vine with it as it came.
She waited while the silence cowered back.
"He was cleaning Old South Church. You know how it is . . .
The rope broke."
                "Now he's up a higher steeple,"
Carl answered softly. "Say he climbed toward heaven
Until whatever force it is that holds us
Bound to our earth got restive after awhile
And yanked him back. He's climbed and clambered now
Right out of sight of earthbound things."
                                        A chunk
Of loose brick clattered on the walk between them.

"I'll have to climb *that* roof," he said, "tomorrow."

Garlic and Sapphires

A fowl, transfixed a moment like ourselves,
Crows without conviction and then descends
From its refuse heap. Aware there is nothing to wait for.

I sometimes wonder if this is what Eliot meant—
The future is not yet here, and the past
Is that area of experience which discloses
The irrelevance of our agreement.

I think also that the river attempts too much
As it sweeps bridges and mementoes of summer nights
Into the Gulf; for the sea, older than the river,
Keeps washing new items up to the beaches,
Bottles, unmated ear-rings, and the scorpion crab,
And particles of sand which attempt new promontories.

WOUNDED KNEE
Two Episodes of the Sioux
Dakota, December 1890

(For Weston, Rowan and Stephen)

Sitting Bull's Death

SIOUX RIDERS, 4TH CAVALRY

I listen with hungry ear
for harness on brown hills,
carbine creak and sliding
leather of troops trotting
down slopes like the rubbed humps
of buffalo, Sioux riders
(Last Horse or Shot to Pieces)
some in a coming summer
to fall far off screening
Rhineward for Abrams' armor.
''Only the stones
can stay on earth forever''
Stands in Timber said.

DAKOTA, DECEMBER 1890

Sitting Bull in on Grand River
south of Standing Rock,
McLaughlin's agency,
as the Sioux wind lapses.
Time now of Ghost Dances
to pound up out of earth
buffalo days again
quickening the hawk hearts.
The agent rides to the Grand,
confronts the chief stooping
to leave his sweat bath lodge.
"You must send your dancers home."
Sitting Bull answers:
First go west together
to Wovoka's desert,
find the Dance Prophet
and hear his Pray.
McLaughlin looks away.
"Such a journey would be
like chasing last year's wind."

From Cuny Stronghold
on the Badlands table
Kicking Bear calls the chief
where his dance-fevered braves
have tied up their ponies' tails.
McLaughlin hears and acts.

When sun rolls off the earth
under undying skies
like plains flooding with night,
they meet at Bull Head's cabin,
thirty Indian police
among them Hunkpapa
of Sitting Bull's own band.
They will seize the shriveled eagle
at his white man's lodge
before first rise of light
led by Lieutenant Bull Head,
rival of Sitting Bull's
head man Catch the Bear,
Red Tomahawk and Shave Head.
While they arrest the chief

Red Bear and White Bird
will saddle his circus grey,
his favorite, Cody's gift.
Now they ride closer in
to Grey Eagle's cabin
and spend slow hours recounting
old Sioux times and raids.
"We all felt bad" Lone Man
recalls years afterward.

Sweet Root brought wisdom once
from Medicine Lodge Butte.
He told the Cheyennes:
"A white people will come
with long hair on their faces
and search the holy hills
to find their medicine stone.
They will tear the earth
and you will tear it with them.
Then you will become crazy,
you will forget my words."

In darkness the Sioux police
mount and at Bull Head's "Hopo!"
trot toward Sitting Bull's camp
through a mizzling chilly rain.
By first light they ford
the Grand and gallop in,
startled dogs yelping up.

Red Bear and White Bear run
to ready the circus grey.
The officers hammer the door.
Inside the chief calls
"How, all right, come in."
While Sitting Bull crawls, puny,
out of his floor pallet
one lights a kerosene lamp.

Cold thin daybreak washes
the wakened village now
ringing police outside.
Their chief comes to the door
Bull Head on his right,

Shave Head at his left arm,
Red Tomahawk behind.
Catch the Bear calls ''Ho!
they come as we expected.
Will you let the Metal Breasts
take you?'' Sitting Bull halts.
''Then I will not go.''
The crowd mills, coils.
Catch the Bear thrusting
a rifle through his blanket
shoots Bull Head who twists
falling and shoots the chief.
Red Tomahawk, pistol drawn
fires pointblank behind him.
Above their slumped leader
skull bleeding in the dirt
Sioux struggle hand to hand.
Lone Man clubs Catch the Bear.
Hostile chiefs Brave Thunder
and Spotted Horn Bull fall.

Among shots and rifle smoke

Sitting Bull's show horse
plunging back on its haunches
performs Wild West tricks
while the warrior Hunkpapa
break away to timber.
"Well, we have killed our chief"
Lone Man says quietly.
Red Tomahawk sends a rider
galloping for Fechet's cavalry.

Sunlight weighs like pollen
golden in heavy air
at Medicine Lodge Butte
rising from long grass plains
outside the holy hills.
"Only the stones
can stay on earth forever"
Stands in Timber said.

41

Wounded Knee

Bear Coat—General Miles—
fearing Spotted Elk may join
Kicking Bear's Ghost Dancers
on Cuny Stronghold,
orders his prompt arrest.

Over windrushed plains
toward the Badlands rigid
in thin December light
cavalry hunt the chief
and his Minneconjou Sioux.
Pneumonia-weak he holds
his horse among the warriors
until at the Badland scarp
he is forced to a jolting wagon.

The last Sioux chief out
Spotted Elk, Great Compromiser,
offered one hundred ponies
by agency Oglalas
to settle their disputes,
rides painfully toward Pine Ridge.

The straggling Minneconjous
evade Sixth Cavalry troops
patrolling east from the Black Hills.
Eluding the Negro Ninth
scouring Cuny approaches
they come to Red Water
and Porcupine, small creeks
flowing northeast of Pine Ridge
the winterbound agency.

Grand River refugees
from Sitting Bull's Hunkpapa
fled without tipis or food
after their chief's death,
reach their meager fires
dreading pursuit by Forsyth
and the Seventh Cavalry,
Custer's old command.

Seventh scouts intercept them,
their sparse column toiling
along the Porcupine,
and call up Major Whitside.

Ringed by troopers and warriors
the major bends from horseback
to Spotted Elk in his wagon—
soldiers in their greatcoats,
yellow-lined capes and caps
of muskrat fur, the Sioux
scanty and lean on their ponies.
Shaking hands Whitside says
"You must go down to Pine Ridge."
The sick chief answers "Yes,
that is where I am going."

Spotted Elk riding
in an army ambulance wagon
watches his Minneconjous
herded like plains cattle
into camp on Wounded Knee.

Bad news comes. Big Road,
Little Wound, Fast Thunder
and five hundred "friendlies"
ridden to Cuny Stronghold

have persuaded the Dancers in,
with game gone far and scarce,
to Pine Ridge and surrender.
More than December light
fades in the canvas wagon
where Spotted Elk in custody
like Crazy Horse before him
grieves at the free life ending.

With daylight Forsyth ranges
Custer's old troop captains
to form a council square,
veterans, all but Nowlan,
of the Little Bighorn battle.
The chief from his tent doorway
watches his warriors called
into the cavalry cordon
to give up their guns.

Sun striking over his eyes,
Spotted Elk half rises
to prop himself on an elbow.

The band's Ghost Dance leader
Yellow Bird, old medicine man,
begins a rhythmic step
weaving among the braves.
Half-deaf Black Coyote
scuffling with a soldier
triggers his rifle. Yellow Bird
throws up a handful of dust.
Braves fire to breach the cordon
and take a pointblank volley.
White Lance through drifting smoke
sees Spotted Elk's head fallen
lifeless to his right shoulder.

Shells shriek from wagon guns
to shred the hundred tipis
ripping women, warriors,
children, running mingled
south toward the ravine,
east to the creek bed.
Blue Whirlwind crawls
with fourteen wounds and lives.

Zintka Lanuni, Lost Bird,
nurses at her dead mother.
In the south ravine Dewey Beard
finds his mother bloodsoaked
carrying a soldier's pistol.
''Pass by me, my son,
I am going to fall down.''
A bullet thuds and fells her.

Between torn lodges
and over December fields
troopers hunt survivors.
Night freezes in
sealed down by winter dark,
ice upon pain. With daybreak
a scattering buckshot blizzard
northers over dry plains
on the Minneconjou trail
across the little creeks,
blinding flattened tipis,

the Wounded Knee slaughtered
and Spotted Elk, half-risen
head fallen to his right,
last chief of the free Sioux.

Note: For facts and circumstances I have relied mainly upon James Mooney's *Ghost Dance Religion* (1896; abridged by the University of Chicago Press, 1965) and Robert M. Utley's *The Last Days of the Sioux Nation* (Yale University Press, 1963). The names Last Horse and Shot to Pieces appeared on the 4th Cavalry roster when I served with it in 1941-2.

CRAZY HORSE

Don't touch me, I am Crazy Horse.

He disappeared, the strange Oglala
out of the small room where they knifed him,
from the heaviness of his final hours
into evening's wounds.

Unlike his killers he felt sunlight first
where skies hang big above meager creeks
and broken washes flowing with long grass
near *Pa Sapa,* the sacred hills.
There on a pony drag
his parents brought his bones.

You cannot sell the earth
on which the people walk.

THE CHEYENNE CREATION

Floats on Water lay
on a lonely water world
where the sun's hot blade
cut ripples of light
or an ice moon circled
flights of arrowing snow.
Dry land was not yet made.
No other live thing stirred
two-legged or four-legged
but gliding water birds.
Floats on Water told them:
"Sharers of this wide water,
look for mud and scoop it
in your bills for me
so earth can be made."
They skimmed water seeking
and winged way off seeking
but found no mud to carry
till a small blue coot
dived down under water
to bring up in its beak
a scoop from the sea bed.
He swam to Floats on Water
who took the mud and dried it
in the slant sun fire.
Then scoop after scoop
as the mudhen dived
Floats on Water shaped
and dried and set the earth.

Heamma-wihio came, the sky creator
down the Stars' Hanging Road

and took from his right side
a rib to make man,
then from man's left side
a rib to make woman.
He set her in the North
white-haired but never ageing
to control Hoimaha,
storm-bringing Winter Man.
He set man in the South
young and also ageless
to control the Thunder
bringer of summer and fire.
Each year Hoimaha
fights against Thunder twice.
At the Moon of Flying Leaves
with cold and sickness Winter Man
charges in snow from the North
pushing Thunder before him.
At the Moon of Red Grass Appearing
with his rains arrows Thunder
drives back Winter Man.

Note: A re-imagining of the creation story which George Bird Grinnell wrote down from oral tradition in *The Cheyenne Indians* (New Haven, Yale University Press, 1923).

THE MAYA CREATION
Book of Chilam Balam

By the counting of footsteps, by the measure
of the footsteps of God departing from the East
naming the day 12 *Oc* that had no name,
before the dawn of the world, by the four lights
they moved from the four layers of stars.

Maternal grandmother, maternal aunt,
paternal grandmother, sister-in-law
asked "Whose are these footprints?" By himself
God moved, by his own effort in the East
created the *uinal,* the twenty days,
created day, as it was called, and earth,
rocks and trees, sea things and land things,
staircase of water and the clouds and heavens.

Days were set in order by that count,
the long count carved upon the stelae
in rain forest among lianas and rain,
jungle eclipse. From the combed pyramid
(Copan or Chichen Itza) from the pure temple
Venus, *tuns* ("vague years") through morning mist.

Out of *Oc,* or footstep, came the names of time.
By the day 13 *Oc* all was created
after forty days, the footsteps from the East.

OSAGE

Descending through oak leaves
came the Sky People
arms upspread like eagles,
tumbling acorns down.

Down to the Middle Waters,
the People from the Stars
set between seasons now—
between ice and sun,
blizzard and funnel wind,
flood river, scorching heat:
torrential rains and light.

Here on the Middle World
fixed in change we wait.

This is Ray Smith's fourth book of poems. It was preceded by *No Eclipse, The Greening Tree,* and *October Rain.*

Mr. Smith has been a teacher and librarian in Iowa, Minnesota, California, and Wisconsin where he now lives in Superior.

He was a recipient of *Poetry* magazine's Guarantor's Prize.